WANDERERS

A WALK THROUGH TIME AND TRANSPORTATION

WRITTEN BY **JULIA MOSS**
ILLUSTRATED BY **TOSHIKI NAKAMURA**

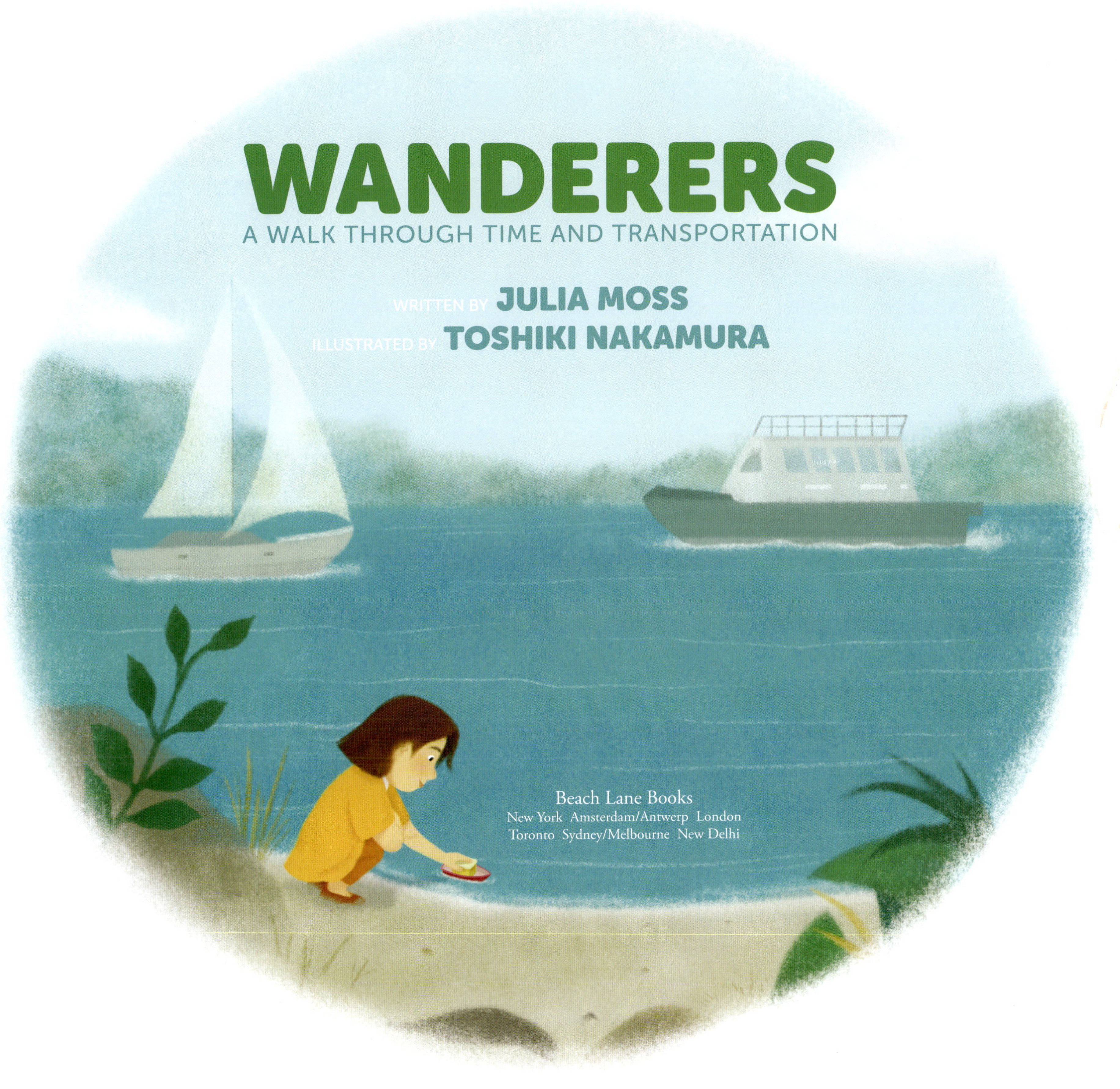

Beach Lane Books
New York Amsterdam/Antwerp London
Toronto Sydney/Melbourne New Delhi

Since the beginning
we've been on the roam,
searching for food, adventure, and home.

First we were walkers.
We hiked and we ran
across mountains and deserts,
through forests and sand.

c. 315,000 BCE: *The first humans evolved and began to travel the world by foot. Walking was the single form of transportation for nearly 270,000 years.*

We sat by the ocean, the rivers, and dreamed
of what lay across. Then we planned and we schemed.
Could we glide on the water with help from a tree?
If we whittled an oar, could we wander the sea?

c. 50,000 BCE: The first watercrafts were likely rafts made of reeds. While we have no archaeological evidence of these early boats, researchers know that humans traveled across a large body of water to reach Australia.

c. 8000–7000 BCE: People crafted the first canoes by digging or burning out the center of tree trunks to create a place for sitting. Remains of these early boats were found in both Nigeria and the Netherlands.

c. 5000–4000 BCE: The oldest-known oars, discovered in China and Japan, were carved using stone tools.

c. 7500 BCE: Humans domesticated dogs to pull carved wooden sleds as they migrated across Arctic regions. The earliest dogsleds were found in Siberia.

c. 6000–4000 BCE: Since walking on snow is slow and challenging, people used wood and animal hide to craft skis and snowshoes, making it much easier to travel long distances.

We traveled to places that glistened with snow
and puzzled together some new ways to go.
How could we wander without falling through?
Could we slide like the seals or balance on shoes?

With our toes in the sand, we watched the birds fly.
New ideas arose as the breeze rustled by . . .

Could we harness the wind if we wove our own sails?
With the stars as our guide, could we wander with whales?

c. 3200 BCE: The first depictions of sailboats appeared in Egyptian artwork. The earliest sails were made from animal skins, cloth made from tree bark, and woven reeds.

c. 3000-1000 BCE: People traveled long distances on double-hulled sailboats across Southeast Asia and the Pacific Islands, using the stars, birds, and ocean swells to navigate.

Back on the land, our meandering roads
felt longer and rougher with heavier loads.

We watched as the animals traveled in stride
and thought to ourselves—could we ask for a ride?

c. 4000–3000 BCE*: As people began trading goods across longer distances, they domesticated animals such as horses, water buffalo, and camels to ride on and carry their loads.*

We tinkered around with a wheel and a pole,
wondering what it would feel like to roll.
If we crafted a cart on two wheels or four,
would it help us to travel and carry much more?

c. 3800–3500 BCE: The transportation wheel was invented in Eastern Europe, modeled after a potter's wheel. People designed carts that could be pulled by animals and used them mainly for growing and transporting food.

c. 2000 BCE: The chariot was created and used for royalty and battle. The earliest artifacts of this two-wheeled vehicle were discovered in Turkey.

1500s: Fashionable horse-drawn carriages were designed in Hungary. This type of travel was so expensive, however, that not many people could afford it.

1826: The original horse-drawn bus line was created in France, making traveling on wheels possible for more than just the wealthy.

Our streets became longer as cities grew wide.
We dreamed up new ways of catching a ride.
Could we fashion a carriage with places to sit?
How far could we go? How many could fit?

Then came a rumble, an echoing *CHOOOO!*
We hopped aboard trains and, oh, what a view!
No need for animals pulling our wheels.
We rushed across countries on rails made of steel.

1825: The first passenger steam train began operation in England, powered by a coal-burning engine. As water was heated by the coals, it turned into steam pressure, which moved the train forward.

Could we travel far distances all on our own,
using only the strength of our muscles and bones?
With some handlebars here and then two pedals there,
we balanced on wheels with the wind in our hair!

1885: The safety bicycle was invented in Europe, modeled after riding on horseback. The exhilaration of traveling fast using only one's own power was revolutionary. For the first time in history, people could chart their own path over long distances without relying on draft animals.

Trains brought us engines and bikes, our own path.
But could we have both? We drew up the math . . .

We tinkered with fuel tanks and bicycle wheels until we invented the automobile!

1886: The first automobile was a large tricycle made from bicycle parts like wire-spoked wheels, gears, and chains, and was powered by a small internal combustion engine. Instead of burning coal like steam engines, this new engine burned gasoline, which expanded when hot, creating pressure to propel the vehicle forward.

Gazing up, we imagined a way we could fly.
Using all that we knew, could we wander the sky?

We crafted propellers, an engine, and wings.
Then *whoosh,* up we soared, high above everything!

1903: The first airplane to take flight was made from wooden frames, cotton cloth for wings, a gasoline-powered engine (like the automobile), and a chain drive (like the bicycle) to power its propellers.

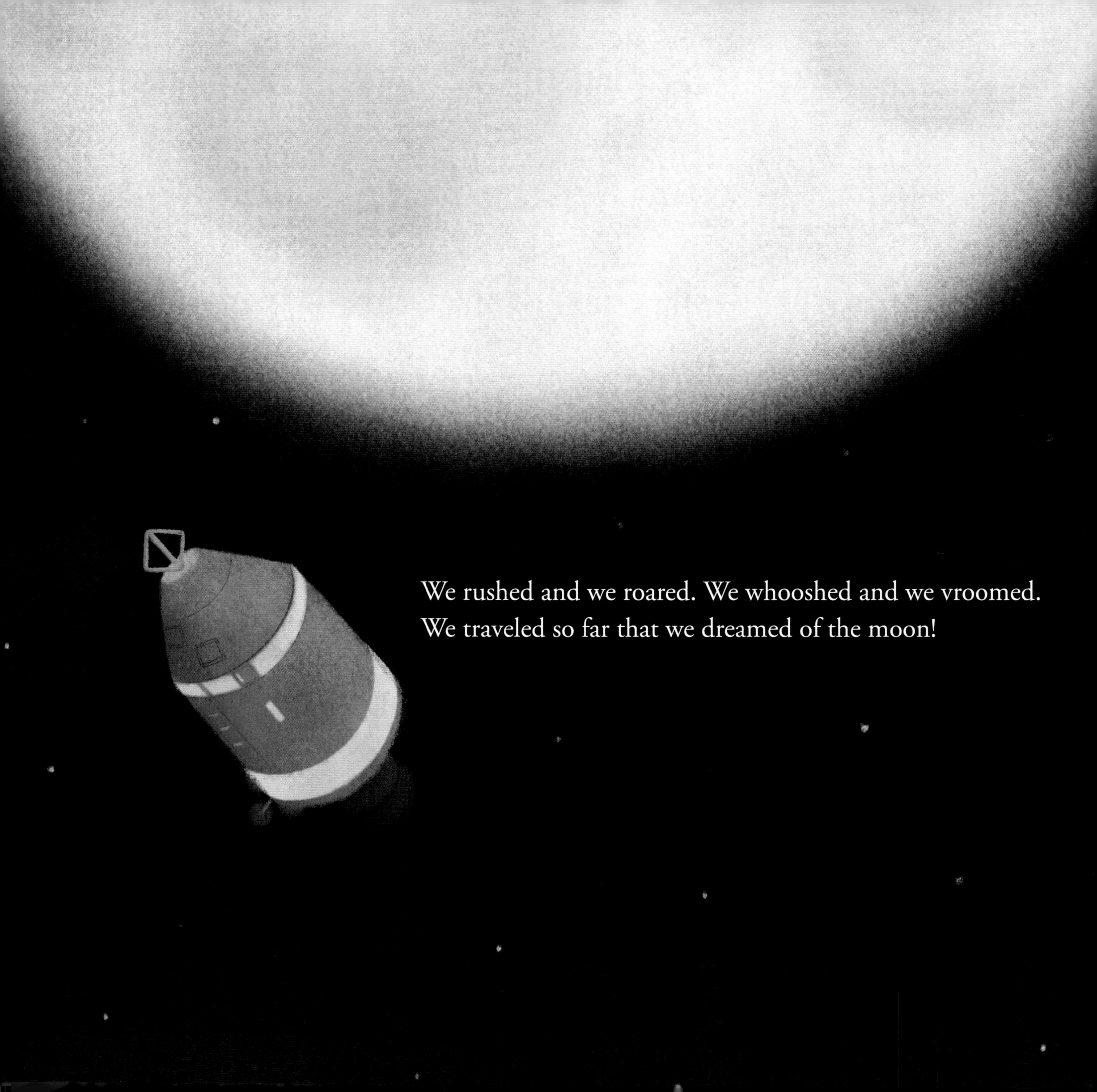

We rushed and we roared. We whooshed and we vroomed.
We traveled so far that we dreamed of the moon!

How could we reach that mysterious place?
Could a rocket ship launch all the way into space?

1969: Humans first set foot on the moon. Since the moon is so far away and it takes a huge amount of power to exit Earth's gravitational pull, scientists built a rocket made up of different parts, each with their own job: launching, fueling, and landing. Once each part's job is done, it detaches from the rocket. Only one small part is for carrying people.

Under sizzling sun, we rethought our tools . . .
Could we go just as far without burning fuel?

What's good for the planet? And what's good for us?
Could batteries power a car or a bus?

While electric vehicles were first invented in the 1800s, gas-powered vehicles became the most popular choice. Scientists later realized that burning fossil fuels like coal and gasoline released carbon into the air, leading to climate change. People are now beginning to choose more sustainable transportation, like walking, biking, and electric vehicles in order to take care of one another and the planet.

We have wondered and wandered
our way through the years.
What's next in our journey?
Which way will we steer?

We'll dream, we'll create,
we'll set out from home . . .

. . . and our hearts will always lead us to roam.

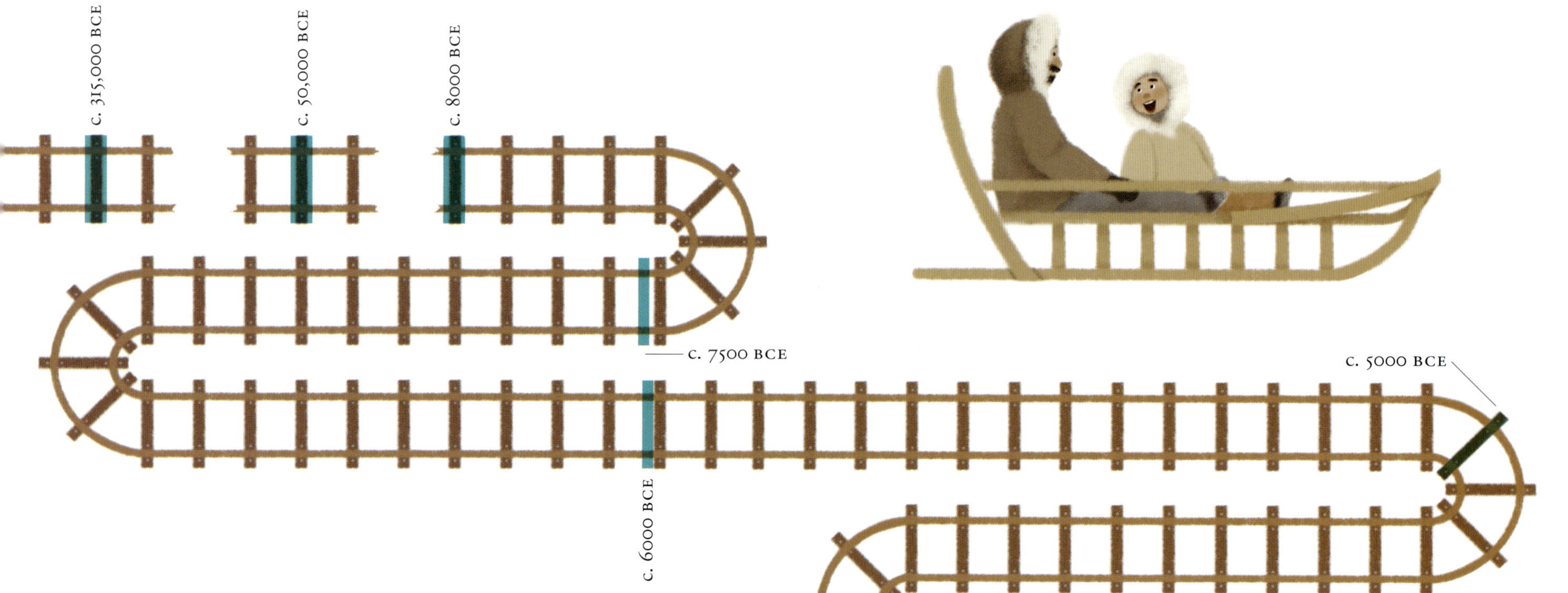

TRANSPORTATION TIMELINE

Our understanding of history is constantly changing as we discover more information. These dates and facts are the best knowledge we have of transportation inventions as of the publication of this book, but they will surely be revised as researchers uncover more of our past. Maybe you'll be a researcher and help us understand our history!

c. 315,000 BCE: The first humans evolved and began to migrate, Africa.

c. 50,000 BCE: People designed the first watercrafts, most likely rafts made of reeds, Australia.

c. 8000–7000 BCE: Earliest-known dugout canoes, Nigeria and the Netherlands.

c. 7500 BCE: Oldest known dogsleds, Siberia.

c. 6000 BCE: First evidence of skis, Russia.

c. 5000–4000 BCE: The oldest known oars, China and Japan.

c. 4000 BCE: First indications of snowshoes, Central Asia.

c. 4000–3000 BCE: People began riding animals as transportation.

c. 3800 BCE: Earliest indication of transportation wheel, Ukraine.

c. 3500 BCE: Oxcarts created mainly for agricultural use, Ukraine.

c. 3200 BCE: The first depiction of a sailboat in ancient artwork, Egypt.

c. 3000–1000 BCE: People traveled long distances on double-hulled sailboats across Southeast Asia and the Pacific Islands.

c. 2000 BCE: Chariots crafted and used mainly for battle, Turkey.

1500s: Traveling by horse-drawn carriage became fashionable, Hungary.

1783: Steamboat created, United States.

1825: First passenger steam train began operation, England.

1826: Horse-drawn buses created, and for the first time in history, traveling on wheels was accessible to everyone, France.

1885: Modern safety bicycle first became widely used, Europe.

1886: Combustion-engine car invented, Germany.

1903: First airplane took flight, United States.

1925: Interstate bus company established, United States.

1964: First high-speed electric rail system, Japan.

1969: First spacecraft to carry people to the moon, United States.

1990s: Modern electric bicycles first mass produced, Japan.

1996: First fully electric car first mass produced, United States.

2010: First fleet of electric buses, China.

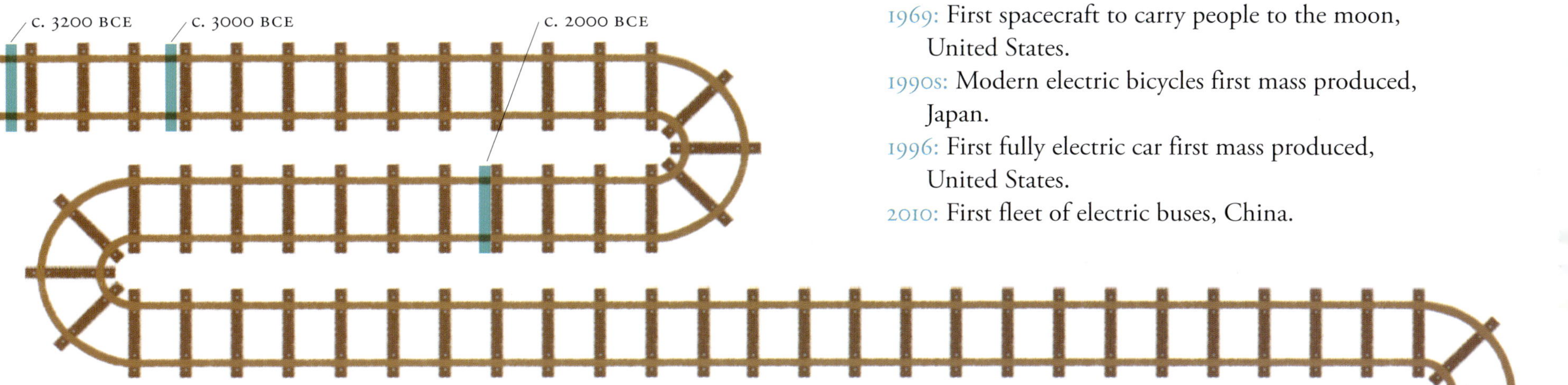

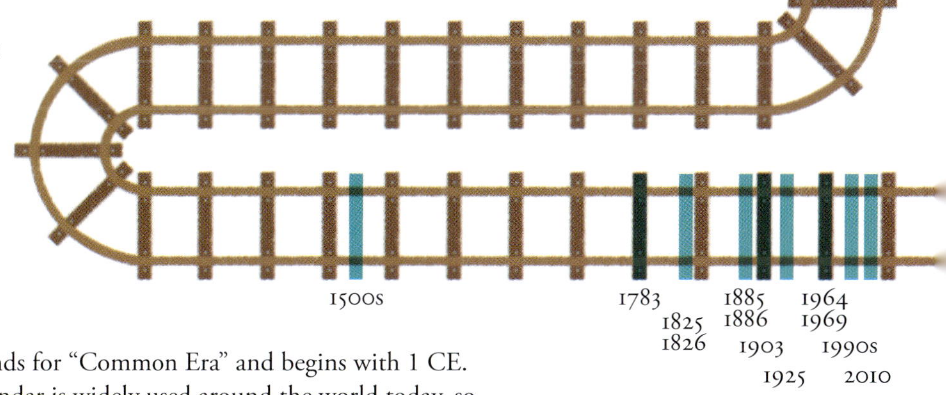

"BCE" stands for "Before Common Era." We use it to talk about things that happened a long time ago, before the year 1 CE. BCE counts backward, so the bigger the BCE number, the farther back in time we are!

"CE" stands for "Common Era" and begins with 1 CE. This calendar is widely used around the world today, so most often we leave off "CE" entirely when writing dates.

"c." stands for "circa," which is Latin for "approximately." We use this to mean that we don't know the exact date, but this is a close estimate.

TOWARD A SUSTAINABLE FUTURE

At every turn of our transportation journey, we have met the hopes and challenges of the moment with creativity and resourcefulness. Those same skills will help us as we grapple with the current challenge of global climate change. How can we redesign our transportation systems to create fewer carbon emissions so that our Earth can be a healthy place to live and wander for generations to come? There are many people working together to answer this question today. Here's how you can help:

Go green: As families and individuals, we can choose to walk, bike, carpool, and take public transit in our daily lives. These modes of transportation release less or no carbon into the air, which slows down climate change and makes the Earth a healthier place to live. How will you choose to wander?

Lead the way: City planners help by designing roads that make it easier and safer for people to walk, bike, and take public transit—all greener transportation options. Do you like to draw and design? What are your ideas for making the streets in your town or city more eco-friendly?

Innovate: Engineers dream up new inventions powered by sustainable sources like solar and wind energy or by human activity like pedaling or pushing. Mechanics make them a reality. Do you like to tinker and invent? What are your big ideas for greener transportation?

SOURCES

Bartels, Meghan. "Humans Started Riding Horses 5,000 Years Ago, New Evidence Suggests." *Scientific American*, March 3, 2023.

Di Piazza, A. *Canoes of the Grand Ocean*. Archaeopress, 2008.

Herlihy, David V. *Bicycle: The History*. Yale University Press, 2004.

Humes, Edward. *Door to Door: The Magnificent, Maddening, Mysterious World of Transportation*. HarperCollins, 2016.

Huntford, Roland. *Two Planks and a Passion: The Dramatic History of Skiing*. Continuum, 2009.

Jackson, Tom. *Machines in Motion: The Amazing History of Transportation*. Bloomsbury, 2019.

Kirkfield, Vivian. *From Here to There: Inventions That Changed the Way the World Moves*. Houghton Mifflin Harcourt, 2021.

Le Page, Michael. "Sled Dogs Are an Ancient Breed Going Back at Least 10,000 Years." *New Scientist*, June 25, 2020.

Paine, Lincoln. *The Sea and Civilization: A Maritime History of the World*. Alfred A. Knopf, 2013.

Standage, Tom. *A Brief History of Motion: From the Wheel, to the Car, to What Comes Next*. Bloomsbury Publishing, 2021.

Stark, Miriam. *Archaeology of Asia*. John Wiley & Sons, 2006.

Watson, Tom. "A Historical Perspective of Snowshoes." *Snowshoe Magazine*. Updated September 22, 2022. Accessed October 31, 2023.

For my little wanderers—Asa, Elio, and Neva

—J.M.

To Kenta, my brother

—T.N.

BEACH LANE BOOKS
An imprint of Simon & Schuster Children's Publishing Division
1230 Avenue of the Americas, New York, New York 10020

The text for this book was set in Adobe Garamond.
The illustrations for this book were rendered digitally.
Manufactured in China
0626 SCP
First Edition
10 9 8 7 6 5 4 3 2 1
Library of Congress Cataloging-in-Publication Data
Names: Moss, Julia (Children book author), author. | Nakamura, Toshiki, illustrator.
Title: Wanderers : a walk through time and transportation / written by Julia Moss, illustrated by Toshiki Nakamura.
Description: First edition. | New York : Beach Lane Books, [2026] | Includes bibliographical references. | Audience: Ages 4–8 | Audience: Grades 2–3 | Summary: "This sweeping, lyrical history of transportation encourages young readers to wonder at human ingenuity while wandering through time and discover some of the coolest vehicles we invented along the way"—Provided by publisher.
Identifiers: LCCN 2025046869 (print) | LCCN 2025046870 (ebook) | ISBN 9781665974578 (hardcover) | ISBN 9781665974585 (ebook)
Subjects: LCSH: Transportation—History—Juvenile literature. | Vehicles—History—Juvenile literature. | CYAC: Transportation. | Vehicles. | LCGFT: Stories in rhyme. | Instructional and educational works.
Classification: LCC HE152 .M67 2026 (print) | LCC HE152 (ebook)
LC record available at https://lccn.loc.gov/2025046869
LC ebook record available at https://lccn.loc.gov/2025046870